Prayers

INSPIRATION and GUIDED MEDITATIONS
for LIVING in LOVE and HAPPINESS

# Prayers

## A Communion with our Creator

### DON MIGUEL RUIZ

#### WITH JANET MILLS

AMBER-ALLEN PUBLISHING
SAN RAFAEL, CALIFORNIA

Copyright © 2001 by Miguel Angel Ruiz, M.D. and Janet Mills

Published by Amber-Allen Publishing, Inc.
Post Office Box 6657
San Rafael, California 94903

Editorial and Production: Janet Mills
Cover Photo and Author Photo: Stephen Collector
Typography: Rick Gordon, Emerald Valley Graphics

ISBN 1-878424-52-1
Library of Congress Control Number: 2001 134014
Printed in Canada on acid-free paper
Distributed by Publishers Group West

10 9 8 7 6 5 4 3 2 1

To the heart of a woman where the divine love
is reflected in the integrity of humanity.
To the mother, the wife, the daughter,
and the friend.

# Contents

Introduction  1

1
Truth  5

2
Forgiveness  15

3
Love  27

4
Gratitude  43

5
Humanity  51

6
Inner Silence  61

7
The Wedding Day  79

8
The Circle of Fire  99

# Contents

❧

## Prayers

Prayer for Truth    13

Prayer for Forgiveness    25

Prayer for Love    35

Prayer for the Physical Body    41

Prayer for Gratitude    49

Prayer for Humanity    59

Prayer for Divinity    77

The Circle of Fire    103

El Círculo de Fuego    121

❧

About the Authors    123

## ACKNOWLEDGMENTS

I WISH TO EXPRESS MY GRATITUDE TO JANET MILLS, the mother of this book, and to Gabrielle Rivera for her valuable contribution.

All my gratitude to our Creator for the inspiration and beauty that gave this book life.

Prayers

Is it not true, my angel of life,
that walking hand in hand into the dream of life
every step is blessed by God?

# Introduction

ALL OF US, AT LEAST ONCE IN OUR LIVES, HAVE FELT a communion with our Creator. There are moments of inspiration when we feel the immensity of creation, the beauty and perfection of everything that exists. Our emotional reaction can be overwhelming. We feel the most wonderful inner peace mixed with intense joy, and we call it *bliss*, or a state of grace and gratitude.

We feel the presence of God.

At other times, we feel overwhelmed by the pressures of life. Everything seems to be going wrong in our lives, and we don't know what to do. We feel too small compared to the immensity of life, and we want to be rescued from our problems. Our emotional reaction might be helplessness mixed with sadness, fear, or anger, and we pray, "Oh God, please help me." We feel that we are being heard; we feel the presence of God, and we are comforted.

Prayer is a communion of the human with the divine. Whether our prayer comes from love, gratitude, and inspiration, or from fear, despair, and desperation, we talk heart-to-heart with divine spirit. In prayer, we quiet all the voices talking inside our heads that tell us why something isn't possible, and open a direct channel to our faith. When we pray we use the voice of the human, but we align with the voice of our hearts, our spirits, and that is what makes the prayer powerful.

To pray is an act of power because it is an agreement between the human and the divine, and we invest our faith in that agreement. Through our faith, we gain the courage to take action, and through action, we move one step closer toward the manifestation of our desires. And when we believe in what we pray for with all of our faith, we multiply our intent.

Prayer fulfills the need humans have for God, for inspiration, for affirmation of our own spirits. In prayer, we communicate with the essence of everything that exists, including our own essence. If we imagine a wolf howling at the moon, that is how we want to pray. We have a message to share with life, with God, and we want to share it with authority.

The message is coming directly from our hearts, we are talking with our own divinity, with God.

The power of prayer can lead us into love, truth, and personal freedom. In this book we intend to use the power of prayer to awaken the love and the joy in our hearts, and to experience a communion with our Creator. May you find love, truth, and freedom in your own personal way.

# 1
## Truth

EVERY HUMAN IS AN ARTIST, AND OUR GREATEST ART
is *life*. Humans perceive life and try to make sense of
life by expressing what we perceive with words, music,
and other expressions of art. We perceive life and then
create a story to justify, describe, and explain our perception and emotional reaction. All humans are storytellers, and that is what makes us artists.

Everything we believe about ourselves is a story we create that is based in reality, but is just our point of view. Our point of view is based on our experience, on what we *know*, on what we *believe*. And what we know and believe is just a program; it is nothing but words, opinions, and ideas we learn from others and from our own life experience. Humans perceive truth, but the way we justify and explain what we perceive is not truth; it is a story. I call this story a *dream*. The human mind mixes perception, imagination, and emotion to create a whole dream. But the story doesn't end there, because every mind of every human mixes together and creates the mind of the planet Earth — the *dream of the planet.*

The dream of the planet is the dream of all humans together. We can call it *society,* we can call it *a nation,* but the result of the creation of the mind, individual and collective, is a dream. The dream can be a pleasant dream that we call *heaven*, or it can be a nightmare that we call *hell*. But heaven and hell only exist at the level of the mind.

In human society, the dream of the planet is ruled by lies, and fear is the result. It is a dream where humans judge one another, find one another guilty, and punish one another. Humans use the power of the word to gossip and to hurt one another. Misuse of the word creates emotional poison, and all that emotional poison is in the dream. It goes around the world, and that is what most humans eat: emotional poison. The dream of the planet prepares newborn humans to believe what it wants them to believe. In that dream, there is no justice; there is only injustice. Nothing is perfect; there is only imperfection. That is why humans eternally search for justice, for happiness, and for love.

For thousands of years people have believed there is a conflict between good and evil in the universe. But this is not true. The real conflict is between truth and what is not truth. The conflict exists in the human mind, not in the rest of nature. Good and evil are the result of that conflict. Believing in truth results in goodness; believing in and defending what is not truth results in evil. Evil is just the result of believing in lies.

All human suffering is the result of believing in lies. To become aware of this is the first thing we must do. Why? Because this awareness will guide us to truth, and the truth will lead us to God, to love, to happiness. The truth will set us free from all the lies we believe in. But we have to experience the truth to know the truth; we cannot put the truth into words. As soon as we start to talk about the truth, as soon as we put it into words, it is no longer the truth. We can experience truth, and we can feel truth, but when we make the story, that story is only true for us. For everyone else, it is not truth. Everyone creates his or her own story; everyone lives in his or her own dream.

To recover awareness is to see life the way it is, not the way we want it to be. To be aware is to see what is truth, not what we want to see in order to justify the lies we believe. If we practice awareness, then the time comes when we master awareness. When we master awareness as a habit, we always see life the way it is, not the way we want to see it. Then we no longer try to put things into words and explain what we perceive to ourselves. Instead we use words to communicate with someone else, knowing that what we are communicating is just our point of view.

God is here. God is living inside you as *life*, as *love*, but you have to see that truth, or there is nothing. You are here to be happy, to live your life, and to express what you are. You were created to perceive the beauty of creation and to live your life in love. But if you cannot find the love inside you, the whole world can love you, and it will not make a difference in you.

Instead of looking to other humans for love, we need to align with our own love, because it's not the love of other humans that will make us happy. What will make us happy is the love we feel for every human, the love we feel for God, for all creation. When the love comes from somebody else, we can feel it and it's nice, but when we feel our own love, it is the best thing that can happen to us. We live in heaven; we live in bliss.

Your body is a living temple where God lives. The proof that God lives in you is that you are alive. In your mind there is emotional poison, but you can clean your mind and prepare yourself for a communion of love with God. Communion means to share your love, to merge in love. And when you pray, it is about communing with the love of God inside you and allowing this love to come out. But if you pray and feel nothing, why waste your time? You need to look inside you and awaken your love. Open your heart and love unconditionally — not because you want love in return, and not because you want to control someone. That is false love. When you love with no conditions, you transcend the dream of fear and become aligned with divine spirit, the love of God, which is the love coming out of you. That love is *life*, and just like the sun, it is shining all the time.

My greatest wish is for all humanity to gain enough awareness to awaken from the dream of fear and use the power of creation to bring heaven on Earth. The entire creation is a masterpiece of art, and just by perceiving the beauty of God's art, our hearts can be filled with joy and contentment.

Use this prayer to increase your awareness of the beauty of all creation, including the beauty of the creation that is you. You are beautiful just the way you are, and when you perceive your own beauty, your emotional reaction is a reaction of love, and you can experience overwhelming happiness. By perceiving your own beauty, you will see yourself in the flowers, the sky, the clouds, the water, and the oceans. But most of all, you will perceive yourself in other humans — in your beloved, in your parents, in your children, in everyone.

Please take a moment to close your eyes, open your heart, and feel all the love that is coming from your heart. Let's join in a special prayer to experience a communion with our Creator.

## Prayer for Truth

TODAY, CREATOR, I ASK YOU TO OPEN MY EYES AND
open my heart so that I can recover the truth about my
life. Help me to resist the temptation to believe the
lies that repress the expression of my life and my love.
Give me the strength to resist the temptation to
believe the lies of others that only create emotional
poison in my heart.

Today, Creator, let me see what is, not what I
want to see. Let me hear what is, not what I want to
hear. Help me to recover my awareness so that I can
see you in everything I perceive with my eyes, with my
ears, with all my senses. Let me perceive with eyes of
love so that I find you wherever I go and see you in

everything you create. Help me to see you in every cell of my body, in every emotion of my mind, in every person I meet. Let me see you in the rain, in the flowers, in the water, in the fire, in the animals, and in the butterflies. You are everywhere, and I am one with you. Let me be aware of this truth.

Today, let everything I do and say be an expression of the beauty in my heart. Let me be aware of the beauty and perfection in everything you create, so that I can live in eternal love with you. Thank you, Creator, for the power to create a dream of heaven where everything is possible. Beginning today, I will use the power of my love to create a masterpiece of art — my own life. Amen.

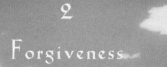

# 2

## Forgiveness

BEFORE YOU LEARNED TO SPEAK, YOU LOVED WITH no effort, you forgave with no effort. It was natural to love; it was natural to forgive. But then you learned how to behave from other people who didn't love, who didn't forgive. Today, if you really want to, you can return to love and let go of whatever is not love. Today can be a new beginning — a day to remember how to love and forgive those who are closest to you.

Imagine that you are in the presence of your mother. Even if your mother is no longer alive, she still lives in your mind. Imagine your mother sitting in front of you so that you can experience a great communion of love with her. Imagine giving your mother the most wonderful hug and kissing her beautiful face. You can feel her emotional reaction to you, and what you feel is love coming from your mother to you. Today, in this moment, you can forgive your mother for any resentment you might have. You don't need to remember what she did or failed to do; you don't need to justify your resentments. To forgive is an act of love, an act of union — to get together again.

Now imagine asking your mother for her forgiveness. Imagine hearing your mother's voice telling you how much she loves you, telling you that she forgives you for whatever you have done. Feel your mother's hand on your face, feel her eyes looking directly at you with deep love and gratitude because she can feel your love. Tell her how much you love her, how much you respect and honor her. Let her know that she has the right to be whatever she is, and that you will never judge her again. Hear her telling you that you can do whatever you want with your life, that she wants you to be happy and enjoy life because you are so wonderful. Imagine her telling you that she is so proud of you, that she loves you and accepts you just the way you are. Perhaps today can be a moment of cleansing, a moment of forgiveness, and through this healing, a moment of love.

Today, if you are a mother or a father, imagine the presence of each of your children in front of you. Feel all the love you have for them, and then forgive them and feel that they also forgive you. Today you can experience a communion of love with your children, a moment of communication, a moment of forgiveness. If you are not a mother or a father, imagine a communion of love with someone close to you whom you need to forgive. What happened in the past is no longer important. What is important is to enjoy the presence of the people you love the most.

Many things can happen in life, many misunderstandings and conflicts. But every time we feel hurt, it is because we believe in something that is not even truth — something that may look like truth, but is not. Believing in lies is how we get hurt; believing in lies is why we distance ourselves from the people we really love. Now is the moment to break free of all those lies and let go of all resentments.

Why not enjoy the people we love the most? Why

spend precious time creating resentments against our parents because we want to be ourselves, and not what they want us to be? Why don't we change our point of view and realize that we have so little time to let them know what we really feel in our hearts for them? Why not put away our pride and ask their forgiveness? It isn't important that we believe they are to blame for some injustice. What is important is to let go of all that pettiness and get together again.

Open your heart, right now, in this moment, and send your love to your parents. Your mother and father love you unconditionally even if they don't show it. If they don't show it, then it is because they are not aware. Your parents bring you the greatest gift, which is life. The message of God is *life*, and that message came to you through your parents. You have given that message to your own children; you have brought them into life. That love is meant to be unconditional, and it *is* unconditional if we don't believe our own lies.

Why do we push our children away because they are not what we want them to be? Why do we push them away with our opinions? They have the right to live their own lives in their own ways. Why not go to your children and tell them, "Forgive me. I didn't mean to push you away. I didn't mean to control your life." When you are kind to your children, they can hardly wait to spend time with you. When you are unkind, you push them away. Why don't you bring them back to you? How difficult can it be for you to open your arms, pull them to you, and tell them how much you love them? Open your heart completely to your children, and accept them just the way they are. Love them *because of* the way they are. It doesn't matter what your children have done; they are your children, and whatever they have done is also because they believe in lies.

Today your relationship with your parents and children can change completely. Let's not waste our lives creating conflict and resentments with the ones we really love when it's so easy to have a wonderful relationship with them. Why do we have to be right all the time and make others wrong? Our opinion is just our point of view, and it is only truth for us; it doesn't mean it is truth for anyone else. We don't have to be right; it is better to be happy than right.

We only have a short time to give all the love that we have in our hearts. Life is so short, and love is too important. We don't know when we will die. We don't know when our parents will die, or when our children, or our spouse, or our brothers and sisters will die. There is nothing important enough in our beliefs to separate us from the people we love. If you knew that you would die tomorrow, would you really want to spend your life in conflict with the people you love? If you had only twenty-four hours to live, how would you write the ending to the story of your life? The angel of death can be the greatest teacher we have, because death teaches us how to be fully alive.

Every day is a day for you to enjoy life, to enjoy the people you love the most, and to let them know that you love them. Today is also a day to honor your beloved, the mother or father of your children. If you respect your beloved, you teach your children how to treat others with respect. If you treat your beloved with kindness and love, that is what your children will learn as they grow up. Our children learn what we do, not just what we say. One of the greatest gifts is to see our children happy in life, to see them expressing themselves and creating a beautiful life. It is a gift to see our children enjoy their children, and to enjoy our grandchildren also. But the best way to teach them is with our own behavior.

Today, why not change how you relate to the people you love? It is a choice that is in your hands, and one that benefits only you. It is a choice that will completely change the quality of your life. Send all your love to your parents, and experience a reunion with them. Send all your love to your children, wherever they are, and bring them back to you. Send your love to your brothers and sisters, to everyone in your family. Choose forgiveness, and communicate with everyone you know, even if they cannot hear you. Wherever they are, they can feel it. Forgiveness is something so important and powerful. Miracles can happen if you just forgive.

Forgiveness is a great expression of love — mainly

for accepting love, beginning with ourselves. Why not love ourselves unconditionally? Why spend our lives creating conflict with ourselves by judging ourselves, rejecting ourselves, or living our lives in shame, guilt or blame? Why spend our precious lives trying to be what we are not, knowing that we never will be? Why not accept ourselves just the way we are, and love ourselves the way we are? The image of perfection we have learned to search for is one of the biggest lies.

Today, in this moment, send all the love in your heart to yourself. Love is your nature; don't resist what you really are. You can improve your life just by expressing what you are, just by following the love in your heart in everything you do. And forgiveness is a great way to give love to yourself. Imagine how easy life could be if you were kind to yourself. Today is a wonderful day to begin a new relationship with you.

## Prayer for Forgiveness

TODAY, CREATOR, GRANT ME THE COURAGE AND THE will to forgive the people I love the most. Help me to forgive every injustice I feel in my mind, and to love other people unconditionally. I know the only way to heal all the pain in my heart is through forgiveness.

Today, Creator, strengthen my will to forgive everyone who has hurt me, even if I believe the offense is unforgivable. I know that forgiveness is an act of self-love. Help me to love myself so much that I forgive every offense. Let me choose forgiveness because I don't want to suffer every time I remember the offense.

Today, Creator, help me to heal all the guilt in my heart by accepting the forgiveness of everyone I have hurt in my life. Help me to sincerely recognize the mistakes I have made out of ignorance, and give me the wisdom and determination to refrain from making the same mistakes. I know that love and forgiveness will transform every relationship in the most positive way.

Thank you, Creator, for giving me the capacity to love and forgive. Today I open my heart to love and forgiveness, so that I can share my love without fear. Today I will enjoy a reunion with the people I love the most. Amen.

3

Love

TODAY YOU CAN TAKE A GREAT STEP TOWARD A return to love by healing your relationship with yourself. Love for yourself is the key to loving others. Love begins with you. When your relationship with yourself is based on love and respect, your relationship with everything in life will change, including your relationships with the people you love.

How do you feel about yourself? Do you love, respect, and honor yourself? If the answer is no, that explains all the broken hearts you have had. When you don't love, respect, and honor yourself, then you allow other people to treat you without love, respect, and honor. But once you learn to treat yourself with love, respect, and honor, there is no way that you will accept anything less from others. If someone wants to play an important role in your life as your friend or lover, husband or wife, then you already know what kind of person you want. It is obvious if that person is not what you want, and you have this awareness right from the beginning. Why? Because you are true to your integrity, and you no longer lie to yourself.

Integrity is the totality of yourself; it is what you really are, not what you believe about yourself or what you pretend to be. When you are true to your integrity, you never consciously go against yourself. You are honest with yourself, and you notice when someone shows you disrespect. If someone treats you disrespectfully, you have the clarity to say, "Hold it. I don't like the way you are talking to me." You put up a boundary right away because you won't allow yourself to be abused. You create a clear system of boundaries with other people, and you also respect the boundaries that others put on you.

With self-love, if someone wants to be with you, that person has to come from love and respect, not from fear and disrespect. If you are already in a relationship that doesn't honor you, then you can enter a period of healing and cleansing so that both of you return to love and respect, beginning with yourself, and continuing with each other. You begin with yourself because you need to have love in order to give love; you need to have self-respect in order to give respect. The relationship needs to be based on respect. If there is no respect, sooner or later there is going to be a broken heart.

What do I mean by respect? If I'm in a relationship with you, I respect your choices; I will not try to control your choices. Because I love you, I allow you to be what you are. I don't have to agree with you, but I respect every belief you have, every choice you make, because I love you the way you are. I also respect my own life, and I will not allow you to control my life. If you don't respect me, I will still love you, but that may be the end. The only way to save our relationship is to recover the respect, to communicate better, and to create new agreements with a new set of boundaries. In this way, the relationship can be healed.

Self-love is something completely different from selfishness. Selfishness says, "If you love me, you have to put up with all my emotional garbage, you have to put up with my anger, my judgments, and never leave me." To tell others that you love them, and then to abuse them, is not love; it is selfishness. How can I love you and abuse you at the same time? For me to keep you, even if I'm abusing you, is selfishness, not love.

Self-love gives you the power to break all the lies you were programmed to believe — lies that say, "I'm not good enough; I'm not beautiful enough; I'm not strong enough; I can't make it." With self-love, you are no longer afraid to face responsibilities in your life, to face problems and resolve them as soon as they arise. Why? Because you can trust yourself completely to make choices that support you, and you never set up circumstances that go against you.

With self-love, you enjoy your own presence. You enjoy what you see every time you look in the mirror, and the big smile on your face enhances your inner and outer beauty. With self-love, you don't have to follow a false image of perfection or try to prove that you are good enough for love.

When you have self-love, you no longer live your life according to other people's opinions. You don't need other people to accept you or tell you how good you are, because you know what you are. With self-love, you aren't afraid to share your love because your heart is completely open.

Today can be the day when you experience the beauty of yourself. Today can be the day when you reconnect with your own spirit and express all the love in your heart. Focus your attention on what you are feeling in this moment. Feel the desire to be alive, the desire for love and joy, the desire to create something wonderful to share with others. The biggest mission you have is to make yourself happy, and to share your love, your joy, and your happiness.

Now let's have another communion of love with our Creator. Feel these words coming directly from your heart to the one who created you.

## Prayer for Love

TODAY, LORD, HELP ME TO ACCEPT MYSELF THE WAY I am, without judgment. Help me to accept my mind the way it is, with all my emotions, my hopes and dreams, and my unique personality. Help me to accept my body the way it is, with all its beauty and perfection.

Today, Lord, clean my mind of emotional poison and self-judgment, so that I can live in peace and love. Let the love for myself be so strong that I never again reject myself or sabotage my happiness and personal freedom. Let me love and accept myself without judgment, because when I judge myself, I find myself guilty, and then need to punish myself.

With the power of self-love, let all my relationships

be based on love and respect. Help me to let go of the need to tell others how to think or how to be. Let me accept the people I love just the way they are, without judgment, because when I judge them and blame them, I find them guilty, and want to punish them. Help me, Lord, to love everything you create with no conditions, because when I reject your creation, I reject you.

Today, Lord, help me to start my life over with the power of self-love. Help me to explore life, to take risks, and to love myself unconditionally. Let me open my heart to the love that is my birthright so that I can share my love wherever I go. Amen.

## Honoring the Physical Body

The physical body is like an animal that is completely loyal to us. It takes us wherever we want to go; it gives us all the pleasures of life: eating, drinking, or just running on the beach and playing. And what do we do? We abuse our physical body, we judge our physical body, we are ashamed of our physical body, and our physical body suffers. Nobody abuses our physical body more than we do. We treat our pet dog or cat better than we treat our own body. We are the ones who are not loyal to our body.

I used to judge my physical body all the time. When I looked at my body in a mirror, I used to think, "Oh no, I don't like it." Can you imagine how selfish it is not to like your own body when your body does everything it can for you? Today, I love my physical body. I'm not ashamed of my body at all. I am generous with my physical body, and I give it whatever it needs.

Your physical body loves you unconditionally. Even if you judge your body, even if you reject it and don't like it, your body is completely loyal to you. Even if your body is getting old or feeling sick, still it is doing the best it can. Just knowing this is enough for you to fill your heart with gratitude for the gift of your physical body.

Today I propose that you start a brand new relationship with your physical body. I propose that you treat your physical body just as you would treat a precious loved one in your life. Stop being selfish with your physical body, and give it whatever it needs to be healthy and happy. Can you do that?

Today is a new day, a new beginning for you to give gratitude to your physical body for everything it does for you. When you learn to love your physical body, every activity can become a ritual of gratitude where you fully express the joy to be alive. Every time you wash your body can be a prayer of gratitude to God. Every time you eat can be more than a prayer; it can be a celebration of life because you are giving food to God so that *life* can keep going. Beginning today, you can change your relationship with your physical body, and your whole life will change.

## Prayer for the Physical Body

TODAY, CREATOR, I PROMISE TO MAKE A NEW agreement with my physical body. I promise to love my body unconditionally as my body loves me. I promise to protect and take care of my body. I will never again reject my body, abuse my body, or be ashamed of how it looks. From now on, I will accept my physical body as it is. I will enjoy my body, and be grateful for all the pleasures of life it gives me.

Forgive me, Creator, for believing all the lies about my physical body. Forgive me for judging my physical body against a false image of perfection. Forgive me for everything I haven't liked about my physical body.

Today, Creator, help me to see my physical body as a living temple where you live. Help me to respect my body, to love and honor my body. I know that to treat my physical body with respect, love, and honor is to respect, love, and honor your creation. Help me, Creator, to give my physical body whatever it needs to live in perfect health, harmony, and happiness with you. Amen.

# 4
## Gratitude

GRATITUDE MUST BEGIN WITH THE ONE WHO CREATED us because we receive the greatest gift from our Creator: *life*. How can we sincerely show our gratitude to God and say thank you from the bottom of our hearts? The best way to show our gratitude is to receive the gift, and give our thanks by enjoying the gift, by living our lives fully and completely.

For many of us, it is easy to give, but very difficult to receive. When we master gratitude, we can easily receive without feeling guilty because we know that by receiving, we give pleasure to the one who is giving. For example, if someone cooks a meal for you, the best way to say thank you for the gift is to really enjoy the food. The one who cooks for you feels pleasure just seeing how much you enjoy it. If you cook a meal for your own children, and you see how much they enjoy your food, you can keep cooking the rest of your life just to feel their pleasure!

The same thing is true with life. Our Creator gives us the gift of life, and the way to say, "Thank you, God, for life," is by enjoying our lives, by living our lives intensely, by being who we really are. Life is passing so quickly. Even if we live one hundred years, life is too short. What will we do with our lives?

Should we spend our lives feeling sorry for ourselves? Should we spend our lives creating conflict with the people we love by judging them, trying to control them, or telling them how we want them to be? Should we spend our lives being afraid to be alive, afraid to express what we are in the world?

The way to express our gratitude for life is by being truly alive, not hiding from life in a corner, or watching life pass us by. The biggest fear we have is not the fear of dying, but the fear to be alive, to be ourselves, to say what we feel, to ask for what we want, to say yes when we want to say yes, and no when we want to say no. To express what is in our hearts is to be truly alive. If we pretend to be what we are not, how can we be truly alive?

To live with gratitude is to enjoy every moment of this precious gift that comes from God. We don't have to say, "Thank you, God," for life; we can show our gratitude to God by living in happiness and love. Gratitude is one of the greatest expressions of love. When we master gratitude, we give our love generously because we know there is no end to our love. Whatever we give, we give with generosity because our Creator is so generous with us. And we know that we are worthy of receiving all that is good in life because we come from God, and God is all there is. If God is everywhere and exists within all things, then how can God withhold life's gifts from God's own creations?

Today is a wonderful day to be grateful, to express all the gratitude that is in your heart. Why not practice gratitude in every moment until you master gratitude, until it becomes a habit? The more you practice gratitude, the more you see how much there is to be grateful for, and your life becomes an ongoing celebration of joy and happiness. When you master gratitude, you perceive God in everything, and your reaction is love and gratitude for the greatest gift, which is *life*.

I suggest that we live the rest of our lives with gratitude and appreciation for what we receive just by being alive. Just being alive, just the pleasure of breathing, is enough to fill our hearts with gratitude.

Now let's have a strong communion of love with our Creator. Feel these words as if they are coming directly from your own heart. Together with one heart, let's send these beautiful words of gratitude to the one who created us.

## Prayer for Gratitude

TODAY, CREATOR OF THE UNIVERSE, MY HEART IS filled with gratitude for the gift of *life* you have given me. Thank you for the opportunity to experience this beautiful body and this wonderful mind. Today, Lord, I want to express my gratitude for everything I have received from you.

I know the way to say thank you for *life* is by fully enjoying every moment of my life. And the only way to enjoy every moment is to love. Today, I will express all the love and happiness that exist in my heart. I will love your creations, I will love myself, and I will love the people who live with me. I know that life is too short to waste in misery and drama with the people I love. I will enjoy the presence of the people I love, respecting their choices in life as I respect my own.

Today, I will graciously receive your gifts by enjoying your gifts, by enjoying the beauty of all your creation. Help me to be as generous as you are, to share what I have with generosity, just as you share your gifts so generously with me. Help me to become a master of gratitude, generosity, and love so that I can enjoy all of your creations.

Today, Lord, help me to manifest my creation as you manifest the universe, to express the beauty of my spirit in the supreme art of the human: the art of dreaming my life. Today, Lord, I give you all of my gratitude and love because you have given me *life*. Amen.

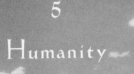

# 5

# Humanity

I BELIEVE IN ANGELS. THE WORD *ANGEL* MEANS *MESSENGER*. Everything that exists is a manifestation of one being, and it manifests through messengers. Messengers deliver the will of the one being, and the supreme messenger is *light*.

Light is alive, and it carries the message of life all around the universe. Light, the divine messenger, has billions of different frequencies. Though it is only one being, it divides itself for the creation of life into our beautiful Mother, the planet Earth. Every vibration of light has a specific message for every kind of life that exists in this beautiful world. There is a specific frequency of light that carries information for the creation of humans. That ray of light manifests as DNA and only creates humans — you and me. We are beings of light because we are beings of energy. The force of life that manifests as humans recognizes its own kind. It is the soul of humanity, and it is a major angel. The soul of humanity is a messenger; *you* are a messenger, and your message is your life.

In your heart is the real message that humans have been trying to deliver. For so many years we have delivered the wrong message: a message of fear, a message of selfishness, a message of anger, violence, and injustice.

This message is not ours. Humans were made for love; our function is to love. Sharing love is human nature because we come from love, we come from light, we come from our Creator. Our nature is to love and to play, to enjoy life, and to be happy.

We have a message to deliver — first to ourselves and then to one another. That message is to remember what we really are, to remember our real nature, and to become what we really are. It doesn't matter where we are born; it doesn't matter what language we speak. We are only one being; we come from the same ray of light, and we have the same message. Our message is love and joy.

You can recover the integrity that you lost as a child. You can recover the message that you haven't delivered for so long, and start delivering it again. The voice of integrity, the voice of your spirit, is always speaking to you even if you don't want to listen. And that voice is saying, "I love you." In every activity of your life, you can express the real message of your heart, the message you are feeling right now. When you express what you really are in life, only beauty can come out of you, only joy and respect and happiness.

Today, imagine all the love flowing from your heart to all the people who need your love. Join your heart with my heart, and together let's offer our love to the world. By putting our hearts together and sending our love to all of humanity, the moment will come when their hearts will react to that love. They will express their love also, the same way that we are expressing our love.

Let's make our love strong, and let's send our love to our homes, to whomever lives with us. Let's bless our homes and let's bless every member of our families.

With these blessings, let's send all our forgiveness to others, and let's receive all their forgiveness in our hearts for any problems that have come between us.

Let's gather our hearts together, and create even more love to send to our community, to our country, to all of humanity. Together let's increase our love until it is so powerful that we can help whoever is suffering in this moment.

Let's send our love to all the children who no longer have parents, to all the children who are being abused. Let's send our love so they can feel the presence of the divine spirit with them.

Let's send our love to the homeless and the poor. Let's send our love to those who are in hospitals, to those who are dying, to those who are suffering physical and emotional pain. Let's send our love to them so that they can feel a touch of spirit in their hearts.

Let's send our love to people who live in jail—no matter what they have done. Let's send our love without any judgment because they are so needy for this love.

Let's send our love where there is war, to all the families who have lost their children and loved ones. Let's send our love to all people who are victims of any kind of disaster in this world, without feeling sorry for them, because that is what they need.

Let's gather our hearts together and make our love grow even stronger. Then let's send our love to all those places where tyrants take advantage of innocent people, to all those places where there is conflict, where humans are abusing humans, so that they can receive a touch of compassion.

Together, by loving all creation, let's offer our love to the one who created us. Let's send our love to the whole world, to every organ of our planet Earth that is in danger — to the forests, to the atmosphere, to the oceans, to wherever it is needed.

I want to send my love to you, to your heart. I want you to take this love and use it for yourself, to stop judging yourself, to stop blaming yourself, to forgive yourself, and to forgive anyone who has hurt you in your life. Then fill your heart with enough love to accept yourself, and to honor yourself as God's creation.

I believe in angels. I believe in you. I believe in myself. I believe in us. Let's deliver the greatest message to the world: the message of our love, the message of our self, our *life*. Together our love will become stronger and more powerful, and if we live our lives with gratitude and love, we will bring heaven on Earth.

Now focus your attention on your heart, on your feelings, and feel the real message of your heart. Feel every word of this prayer in your heart as we have a communion of love, a communion of joy with our Creator.

## Prayer for Humanity

TODAY, LORD, HELP ME TO DELIVER THE REAL MESSAGE of humanity: the message of joy and love. Help me to deliver this message to my own mind, to that part of me that is always judging and abusing me. Let me deliver this message to that part of me that judges other humans. Beginning today, help me to free my mind from all the false messages I deliver to myself, to every human, to every life form on this beautiful planet.

Today, Lord, I will manifest your love in every word I express, in every action I take, so that everything I do becomes a ritual of love for you. I love you so much that I can see you everywhere. There is no way you can hide from me because my love will always find you.

Beginning today, I will respect every creation and treat every creation the way I respect and treat you. I will see you in the eyes of all humans — behind their masks, behind the images they pretend to be. I will respect the *life* that manifests through me, so that every time I see myself in the mirror, I see the beauty of your manifestation.

Thank you, Lord, for creating me, so that I can perceive the beauty of your manifestation. Thank you for giving me an emotional body, so that I can be in ecstasy just by feeling your divine presence. I know that you are my life force, my Creator. Together we can create the most beautiful dream — a dream of love and peace and joy. Together we can create heaven on Earth, to the eternal happiness of humanity. Amen.

# 6
## Inner Silence

I WANT YOU TO FOCUS YOUR ATTENTION ON YOUR inner silence, a place inside you that is the origin of everything that you are. It is a space between you and you, a little space of creation, a little space of multi-dimensional choices, where the dream of life begins.

Relax your body completely. Let go of any tension. Let go of any problems that you have in your life. Let go of any thoughts or judgments. Let go of everything, and give yourself permission to be present in the eternal now. This is a moment to disconnect from the rest of the world, to detach from reality as you know it.

Ignore any noises around you. Get as comfortable as possible, so that you don't need to move. We are going to test your will against the temptation to move your body. Which is stronger — your temptation or your will? Once you are still, you may be tempted to move, to adjust your body or to get up and see what is happening around you. Use your will and do not move. Even if you feel a fly on your face, don't move, don't scratch! The only thing moving should be your lungs. If your will is strong, you will not move.

Once you are still for a while, you may start to feel different body sensations. Perhaps your head will feel big, or your legs and arms will feel strange. If you begin to have these feelings, you are close to stopping the mind from thinking. Between the end of one thought and the beginning of the next is a space. In that space, you will find your inner silence. Inner silence is a place of choice, where every thought in the mind is created. It is the place where dreaming begins — a place where you can witness the creation of thought.

Once you find the inner silence in your mind, all of your senses will start to awaken. Perhaps you will hear birds singing and feel a sense of communion with the birds. Maybe you will hear the rain and experience a communion with the rain. You might hear beautiful music, or just silence and the beating of your heart. Feel yourself perceiving these sounds, creating beautiful emotions inside you.

Now focus all of your attention on your lungs. Imagine that only your lungs and the air exist. Feel the air in your lungs as you never have before. Notice your emotional reaction every time you inhale. You and the air share the most wonderful communion.

Breathe in slowly, so you can feel the air expanding your lungs. Feel the pleasure as the air enters your lungs. Prolong that pleasure by inhaling very, very slowly, and then keep the air inside your lungs until you feel the need to expel the air.

Exhale very, very slowly, so you can feel the pleasure as you allow the air to leave your lungs. Keep expelling the air until you need to inhale again. Breathe in slowly again until you cannot inhale anymore, and then release the air slowly. Every time you inhale and exhale, feel the pleasure of being alive, the pleasure of breathing. It is something so simple that we take for granted every moment of our lives.

Now I would like you to focus your attention on

your emotions. Imagine that the air is made of love. Every time you inhale, love is filling your lungs and every portion of your chest cavity. Your emotional reaction is to accept all the love entering your body, and you react by loving that wonderful connection. You are not afraid to receive all that love, and you enjoy it as you never have before. Prolong this pleasure by expanding your lungs to the maximum, until you have the need to exhale.

Breathe in slowly again, and as the love fills your lungs, let it overflow into your heart. Open your heart, and let the love fill your heart. When your heart is filled to the maximum, feel the love going through your veins and arteries and filling every part of your body. Imagine a complete healing for your physical body and your mind.

Every time you inhale, imagine all that love going

directly to your heart and circulating through your body, cleansing every emotion and every concept in your mind. Feel the love enter every cell, every organ, and every possible space. Feel your entire body being purified and cleansed. Picture the love cleansing whatever toxins exist in your body — whatever pain exists in your body. See your blood carrying off all the things that no longer serve you.

Inhale all the love you can possibly take in, then exhale everything you no longer need. Use all the love that exists outside you to awaken all the love that exists inside you. Inhale all the love again, then exhale slowly, and send all your love to the world, without any resistance. Imagine that you are not afraid to give all your love to the world. Your love is so great that you can send it to the entire world and still it is endless.

Keep using your imagination, and now imagine

that every one of the atoms in your body is a tiny star. Imagine your body as an entire universe made of billions and billions of little stars. Imagine that everything in creation is made of stars. Only stars and the space between the stars exist.

The space between the stars is much larger than the space the stars themselves occupy, but that space between the stars is not empty; it is filled with light. That light contains the force that moves the stars, and gives shape and form to atoms, to molecules, to everything. Light carries all the wisdom and information of the universe. Light is a messenger, and the message is *life*. It is *life* that creates the stars; it is *life* that creates the atoms in our body; it is *life* that is the messenger of the word. *Life* is a force; it is pure energy, and it is the *real* you.

Imagine that you are *life*, and you are passing through everything, everywhere. You are always in action, always transforming. Imagine yourself as a newborn infant growing up in front of your eyes, becoming a little child, a young adult, a mature human, an old human, an empty body without life, without you. Imagine that you are the force that makes the whole process happen, the force that acts on every kind of species in the universe: every human, every fish, every plant, every tree.

You are the force that opens a rose. You are the force creating the thoughts in your mind. You are the force creating your whole dream through knowledge and imagination, memory and emotions. Without you, without *life*, the whole dream dissolves and awareness disappears. You are pure awareness, and physical matter is a mirror for the light that is *life*. Without you, your body would just collapse and disintegrate. But you, the life force, are eternal.

Now imagine that *life* is the same force as *love*.

Inhale, and exhale. With each breath, the love from the stars merges with the love between all the atoms in your body and becomes one. Every time you inhale, your lungs expand, and all the stars of your body expand. Every time you exhale, your lungs contract, and all the stars of your body contract. The microcosm and macrocosm are one being. With every breath, all the stars in the cosmos expand and contract with the same rhythm as the stars in your body. Feel the connection between the rhythm of your lungs, and the expansion and contraction of the cosmos. This is the communion of love between you and God.

Since you were born, and even before, you have been interacting with *life*, with God, or what we can also call *divine spirit*. When you imagine that you are your lungs and that the air is made of love, the only thing you breathe is divine spirit. When you perceive light, everything you perceive is divine spirit. Everything you hear and everything you feel is divine spirit. Perhaps you never noticed that you are only interacting with divine spirit, because divine spirit is the only thing that exists.

Feel your relationship with divine spirit, the one who creates you. Every breath is the most wonderful act of love with divine spirit. Every time you inhale, divine spirit goes inside you, and you merge with divine spirit, becoming one. All the love that you feel is divine spirit going inside you and possessing you. Every time you exhale, your love is so intense and profound that you go inside divine spirit and merge into one. And you no longer know if you are the lungs or the air — if you are you, or you are the divine spirit.

Keep using your imagination, and imagine that the interaction of love between you and divine spirit is how you were created. Imagine that the merging of the breath between you and divine spirit is how everything in the universe was created.

In the beginning, the only thing that existed was divine spirit. It was formless, peaceful, and full of unconditional love. There was only infinite darkness because there was no mirror for it to see itself. Divine spirit could feel itself, and it felt wonderful, but then it had a strong desire to see itself. So it created you, and it could see itself in you because you are the mirror. You reflect its beauty, and as soon as it sees you, its heart is so full of love for you that it has the need to merge with you. Then you merge, and as soon as you merge, it is alone again, but it remembers your beautiful face, and it misses you. Divine spirit wants to see you again, and the desire is so strong that it creates you again, and it sees your beautiful face again, and its love is so strong that it has the need to merge with you. Then you merge, and it is alone again. It is missing you, and its desire is so strong that it creates you again. Then you merge, and there is creation, and you merge again, and again, and again.

When divine spirit is matter, it feels the ecstasy of God passing through it. When divine spirit is formless, it *is* that ecstasy passing through matter, giving it form. Divine spirit, the light of God, is coming and going, manifesting and unmanifesting. This is the rhythm of life, the verse of love. This interaction is how *life* creates the stars, how *life* creates matter — and matter becomes the mirror that reflects the light. Matter is an eternal reproduction of light. And we, *light*, we, *God*, manifest in billions of different creations to explore and celebrate *life*.

All of your life, without even knowing it, you have been interacting with divine spirit to co-create a world of illusion: the *dream* of your life. You were born a great magician, and with the gift of magic you create your personal story. In your personal story there are hundreds of characters, but mainly the story is based on you. The rest of the characters help you to justify your interactions with divine spirit.

Inner silence, that space between thoughts, is the place where you can witness the creation of different images in the mind. Inner silence is the place of silent knowledge where you know everything, and you can see that there are multiple choices. This is the beginning of dreaming, and from this place you can begin to direct the dream.

Nothing is impossible for *life*. *Life* has the power to create anything without limit. And because you are *life*, then just like magic, you can change the dream of your life. From this point of view, you can shift your awareness from your reasoning mind to the reality of light and love itself. With just this simple shift of perception, any dream you can dream becomes possible. And not only is it possible, it is easy for you to modify the dream. You don't need to live in a nightmare anymore; you can live in heaven. It is your choice. You can use inner silence to begin letting go of everything you believe about yourself.

Just imagine what you could do if you really believed that you are *life*. Imagine the possibility of what you could do with the awareness that you are a manifestation of God. It is not just a theory. You are *life*. You are that force that is creating the dream in your mind; you are that force that moves your physical body. But you are not just your physical body; your physical body is just the way you manifest the light of God in this reality. *Life* exists without matter as we know it, in all different forms, and in other realities. There are millions of different realities, and because you are *life*, you can manifest through any of the realities that exist in the universe.

Open yourself to the possibility of a brand new relationship with God — one that begins with awareness. With awareness, it is possible for you to perceive divine spirit, to understand that everything in existence is an expression of God. There is only you and God; there is nothing else. Feel the presence of divine spirit in your physical body. Feel the *life* that is alive in you. That *life* is God.

## Prayer for Divinity

THANK YOU, CREATOR, GIVER OF *LIFE* ITSELF, FOR THE gift of awareness you have given me. Thank you for everything I have received this day, especially for the freedom to be who I really am. I know that I am divine spirit. I know that I am the force that is *life*, the manifestation of your power that becomes the life of humans. Help me to recover my divine consciousness and to humbly accept my own divinity.

Today, Creator, is a wonderful day for a love communion with you. I know that I am an expression of your divine love. Let me accept your love because I am worthy of your love, because you created me, and you only create perfection.

Today, Creator, I will use my life to express your will and to share my joy wherever I go. Thank you for the opportunity to imagine what could be if I shift my awareness and accept my own divinity. Amen.

# 7

# The Wedding Day

TODAY COULD BE THE BEGINNING OF A NEW LIFE FOR you. Today could be a special day to express what you have in your heart.

Imagine that today is your wedding day. You are getting married, and the expectation of joy and happiness is in your heart. Imagine that you are the bride and that the man you will marry is the perfect partner for you. He is exactly the kind of person you have always dreamed of marrying. All is perfect, and you want to be ready for this union.

What does it mean to be ready for this union? How are you going to treat the one you love so much? How are you going to treat someone who allows you to express yourself completely, who respects your freedom, and who doesn't have the need to control you? How will you treat someone who loves you just the way you are, and not just the way you are, but *because of* what you are; someone who never mistreats you or speaks unkind words to you; someone who respects you so much that you can be whatever you want to be, do whatever you want to do, feel whatever you want to feel?

Are you ready for this relationship? Can you allow your beloved to be himself, without any judgment?

Can you love him just the way he is, without trying to change him? Can you respect your beloved so much that you never have to tell him how to be, what to be, what to believe, what not to believe? Can you love him so much that you never put restrictions on the expression of his life, on the expression of his spirit? Are you able to love this way?

Are you ready for this wedding? Can you love and give your love just the way your beloved does? Can you live the rest of your life in complete communion with love, so that you love for no reason? Can you devote your entire life to love, so that every expression of your life, everything you say and do, is because of love?

Just like a marriage with your beloved, being married to love is a choice. Living your life with love is a choice. Close your eyes for a moment, and imagine how you would relate to the rest of the world if love was always moving through you. Imagine what you would say, what you would feel, what you would do, if love was moving through you. Imagine how you would relate with your mother or father, your spouse, your son or daughter, your friends, your boss or co-workers, with anybody on the street.

Imagine that today, your wedding day, will change your life forever in every way. Imagine living your life without judging or blaming other people. Because you love, you never speak against anyone; the urge to gossip is over. You have nothing to say but words of love about everyone. With the eyes of love, your whole reality has changed; everything looks beautiful to you. With the eyes of love, you see the greatness in all the people around you. It doesn't matter what is coming out of their mouths; you can see what is behind all their emotional wounds — behind the anger, the hate, the jealousy.

And you can see that all those emotions coming out of them are just the result of being abused — mostly by themselves, because of little or no self-esteem.

Imagine how you would treat yourself if love was moving through you all the time. What would you think about yourself? What judgments would you have about yourself if love was moving through you? If you began to treat yourself with love, can you imagine all the changes that would happen, just like magic, in your life? You would hardly be angry anymore. You would never be jealous of others. There is no way you could ever feel hate. Right away you would let go of any anger left in your mind against anyone who had ever hurt you. You wouldn't even have the need to forgive anyone, because there would be nothing to forgive. Your mind would be completely healed if love was moving through your mind.

Now remember your life before you were married to love. Where was the self-respect? How many times did you judge yourself and make yourself feel badly? How many times did you speak against yourself — not only to yourself, but to other people also? What kinds of limitations did you place on the expression of your life? How did you treat your beloved before you married love? Where was the respect for the one you supposedly love? How many times did pride push you into conflicts with the people you love the most? If you can see the way you treated yourself and everyone else before you were married to love, you will surely renounce that kind of life and accept love in your life.

During a baptism, the minister might ask, "Do you renounce Satan? Do you accept God?" I'm asking you something similar. Do you renounce the way you used to treat yourself? Do you renounce the way you judged yourself and found yourself guilty, and punished yourself and everyone else? Do you accept love in your life? Do you accept that you can live in an eternal romance with God? That is the real meaning of the baptism: a marriage with God. But we can also call it a marriage with *love*. When you allow your heart to be filled with love for yourself, your life changes completely. You are no longer the same because you renounce fear, anger, sadness, jealousy. You renounce suffering and emotional drama, and you accept love and joy in your life. And what you find is that you don't need to try so hard to be happy. Your life becomes easy, wonderful, and beautiful.

This could be the most wonderful day of your life. Today could *really* be your wedding day: the day you have a reunion with yourself — the *real* you. It sounds very simple, and in fact, it *is* simple. We make it difficult because we are the ones who limit ourselves. We are the ones who make our lives impossible, and then blame everyone around us: our families, our friends, the government. Sometimes we even blame God. But we are the ones who create a living nightmare for ourselves. We don't have to live our lives this way. There is another way of being, another way to relate to ourselves and to everyone else, and that way is love. To love is just a choice. We choose love, or we choose fear; we cannot serve two masters.

Humans claim to have free will, but is that really true? To have free will means that we have the power to make a choice. If we have the power to make a choice, are we really choosing to fight with our parents? Are we choosing to live a life of drama with our beloved or our children? Is that really our choice? Is it our choice to be angry or jealous? Is it our choice to say things that we don't want to say, and later feel guilty because we said this? Is it our choice to do things that we don't want to do, and then feel guilty because we did it? Is that really free will?

I can assure you, if we have free will, if we really have the *power* to make a choice, the only choice is God. The only choice is love and joy and happiness. If we don't make that choice, we don't have the power to make the choice, which means that we no longer have free will. But we can recover free will, and it isn't difficult to recover unless we make it difficult. If our life is not working, it is because of us; it is not because life is hard. If our relationship is not working, it is because of us; we cannot blame the outside.

Today could be the most wonderful day of your life. Today is the perfect day to reevaluate your relationship with yourself. It is the perfect day to reevaluate your relationship with your beloved, with your mother and father, your children, your friends, your job or business, your boss or employees. It is the perfect day to reevaluate your relationship with God. Today could be your wedding day. Are you ready for matrimony?

⌘

I want to share a personal story with you. There was a time when I had forgotten what I was. I really didn't know what I was, and I felt that I had to justify my existence. When I was a teenager in high school, I attended a philosophy class. The teacher said that for thousands of years philosophers and thinkers had tried to explain the meaning of life. The teacher had great opinions about the meaning of life, and he spoke with so much authority that everyone believed him. Then he told us, "You have to find the meaning of life. Only if you find the meaning of life can you find happiness." What a lie, but it sounded good, and I believed him. I tried to find a meaning for my life, something to justify my existence so that I wouldn't die without anyone knowing that I had ever existed.

I searched for many different meanings of life until I was so confused that I no longer knew what I was looking for. I tried to be the best in everything; I would not settle for less than the best. I went into sports and tried to prove myself. I even signed a contract with a professional soccer team in Mexico. But then, at a certain point, I had to make a choice between medical school or professional soccer. I chose medical school because it had more meaning, more importance. I got lost in medical science; I got lost in all that personal importance. I was missing life by trying so hard to find the meaning of life.

Then one day my whole life changed. I met the love of my life, my greatest teacher, the angel of death. She was very beautiful, and believe it or not, she used to come to me in my dreams. I knew that one day I would meet her physically in the flesh, and I also knew that when I saw her, I would have no chance.

I created an entire mythology about the angel of death — my teacher, my lover — and I gave myself to her completely, because this was the only way that I could experience the extreme pleasure of *life*. The angel of death taught me a lot, and I gave up many of my old beliefs. Then one day, in my mythology, I met someone even better than the angel of death. I told myself that the angel of death must have prepared me for my wedding with my true love. This was it. I had to get married, or she would never accept me. But there was only one way to marry her, and that was with unconditional love. Was I ready for this marriage? I wasn't sure that I was, but the angel of death told me, "Yes, you are ready. You have nothing to lose."

Then, with all my courage, I proposed to the angel of *life*, to God, and she said yes. Can you imagine marrying God? Well, I was certainly not the first one to marry God. There are many religions in which people renounce the world and marry God. For me it would be the same; if I married God I had to renounce my world, my old dream. I loved God unconditionally, in all her manifestations. How could I go to God with my old beliefs, my old story?

In the new story, if something is not working in our relationship, it is obviously because of me. How can I blame God? God is perfect; she is wonderful; she is beautiful. When I go to the top of a mountain, and I see the beauty of her manifestation, I know that she is the greatest artist ever. Every creation has my love and respect. I honor and enjoy God's creation, but I can never own it, because everything belongs to her. I know that God loves me just the way I am, and if she loves me just the way I am, then why not love myself that way? How can I judge myself unfairly or hurt my physical body? If I mistreat myself, I mistreat God's creation.

I know that this physical body will die someday. The angel of death can take it right now if she wants to, and I will have no regrets because my story is complete. If she keeps me here, well, I have an extra day to enjoy my honeymoon with God. My story is so romantic; I live in a never-ending romance with God. I am so in love with her that I see her face in every flower; I see her face in every person; I see God everywhere. I know that when the angel of death takes my physical body, I will still be with God. I have no doubt at all. How can I be afraid to die when I have complete faith in God? And if something bad happens to me, it has nothing to do with God. I see it as a gift because it gives me an opportunity to explore another part of life. I only see perfection because God is perfect.

God created us to be storytellers, to be dreamers. My faith is invested 100 percent in this story, and I believe it because I want to believe it. If I'm going to create a story anyway, and if I have a choice of stories to create, I don't think I can create a better story than that one. And guess what? In my story, you are also God's wife or God's husband.

This is my mythology, and by believing this beautiful story, I live my life in the most wonderful fantasy, the most wonderful dream. I know it is just a story, but I can remember the story I used to believe before the angel of death came to me. That story was not truth either, and there is no way I want to live in that story or believe in that story anymore.

I only see God, and I love her so much that she cannot hide from me. If she loves me, good; if she doesn't love me, good. But I believe she loves me, and I believe I am worthy of her love. Why not? Long ago, I used to believe that I wasn't worthy. How odd this seems to me now. Everyone is worthy. If you don't believe you are worthy of love, you are believing a lie.

The angel of death will prepare you for your wedding day by allowing you to see the beauty of *life*. Can you handle God? Can you handle all that love? Imagine yourself on the top of a mountain, merging with God, with all that beauty, with all that love. Wouldn't you like to keep that love for the rest of your life? Wouldn't you like to live like that always?

You were created to react emotionally to the

beauty of creation. You were created to live in bliss and harmony with the entire creation. But your story won't let you live in that bliss, and my story keeps me in that bliss because every habit, every routine I have is to love, to enjoy life, to give 100 percent of myself to make any dream come true. And I have no ambitions really, except to continue creating this beautiful story, and to share it wherever I go.

Today could be the greatest day of your life, the day you finally change your story. Today could be your wedding day; but to be ready for your wedding, you have to take care of unfinished business. You have to say "I love you" to all the people you love, and let them know that you want them to be happy. To be happy they need to be forgiven by you; they need to *feel* that you forgive them. You don't need to call them by phone, and you don't need to suffer in this process either. To suffer is just a choice. To be happy and to live in a divine romance with life is also a choice.

❦

In all the mystery schools, the wedding day is called *the fire ceremony.* The fire ceremony is the moment of enlightenment when we merge with *life*. It is the marriage with the one who created us, and therefore the day when the divinity returns to us.

Close your eyes for a moment, and get very comfortable. Imagine that you are ready for your wedding. Imagine that your heart is full of love. Your beloved, God, is waiting for you at the altar, and you have only a few minutes to surrender to the love in your heart. You are going to devote yourself to the most wonderful relationship, to your union, or reunion, with the one who created you.

Imagine your love radiating through the beautiful smile on your face, through your eyes, and through your heart. Feel your heart screaming, "I do. I accept you, God. I accept you, love. I do." Give yourself completely to the goodness of love, and with that love, let everyone in your life know how much you love them. Just saying "I love you" is enough for you to experience your own divinity.

Imagine the force of *life* passing through your physical body. You feel a communion of love with the Creator, and you are ready to share the joy of your union with everyone. From now on, your life represents a union with God. Your *life* is devoted to love; your *life* is devoted to joy and happiness. This is heaven on Earth, and it is in your hands. Heaven on Earth is a wedding where God is the groom and you are the bride, and you live an eternal honeymoon.

## 8

## The Circle of Fire

THIS BEAUTIFUL PRAYER IS CALLED "THE CIRCLE OF Fire." "Circle" because it represents earth; "fire" because it represents spirit. More than a prayer, "The Circle of Fire" is an agreement of matrimony with God, our Creator. We are proposing a new relationship with God, and it's not important whether God accepts it or not, although surely God will. What is important is that we accept the agreement in our half of the relationship, that we do our part, that we live our lives following this agreement.

If we invest our faith in this prayer, if we follow this agreement, we can create heaven on Earth. To practice this prayer is enough for us to live in happiness and love always. It is something so simple and easy to do. But it's not enough for us to say the prayer; we have to *live* the prayer. To live the prayer is to align our intent with our word, to put our faith in our word, and to feel the reaction in our emotional body. Our emotional body perceives the meaning of our word, it reacts to our word, and the reaction is love coming out of us. In that reaction, we recover our divinity, we put our trust in God, and our whole life changes.

Get very comfortable, and close your eyes for a moment. Take a deep breath, and quiet your mind completely. Say this prayer very, very slowly, word by word, with your heart in every word. Feel all the power in this prayer, all the love and intent. Open your heart, and let all your love come out. Don't resist your emotions; don't resist your love. Let go, and prepare yourself for a communion with our Creator.

# The Circle of Fire

[State today's date]
The day of the Lord
when the divinity returns to me
when living my free will, and with all the power of my spirit
I decide to live my life in free communion with God
with no expectations

I will live my life with gratitude, love, loyalty, and justice
beginning with myself
and continuing with my brothers and sisters

I will respect all creation
as the symbol of my love communion with the One who created me
to the eternal happiness of humanity

Living this prayer is about being alive, being in love, being who you really are. That is the purpose of this prayer. You can change the story of your life at any time. You are the artist, and your art is your life. Every word in this prayer has the intent to heal your mind completely. It can heal every wound in your emotional body, and help you detach from whatever keeps you in drama and suffering. With this information, let's say the prayer again, step-by-step this time, so you can perceive the meaning of each phrase.

*State today's date. . . .*

The purpose for saying the date is to be present in the eternal now. Today, this moment, is the eternal now. There is no past, there is no future. Time is an illusion; life is an eternal present moment. Today is the day of creation, and this moment is the moment of creation.

By saying the date, you announce that today is the day you make a new agreement. What happened a week ago or an hour ago doesn't matter. What matters is your intent in this moment, what you are feeling in this moment of creation. It is a decision that you make today, and it is an ongoing choice that you make every day, in every moment. If you want to add the time of the day, you can do that too, because you don't care about five minutes from now, or an hour from now. If you break the agreement an hour from now — okay, you break it. But then you make the agreement again, and you keep making it again and again until you don't break it anymore.

*The day of the Lord. . . .*

Every day is the day of the Lord, because only the Lord, our Creator exists. You have recognized the day of the Lord, and you believe in the Lord with all of your faith. On this day you are making a commitment to God, and it is an act of power.

*When the divinity returns to me....*

This means when you recover the awareness of what you really are: the one who is creating this moment. This is the day of your illumination, when you recognize your divinity and merge with the only being that exists. You, the human, awaken and reunite with the real you, with God. Whoever you thought you were is gone, and it has gone to divinity. You accept responsibility for your divine self, and in this moment, you recover your faith, you recover your authority, and everything is possible. You have authority over yourself, over your own life. You claim the right to be alive, to express yourself in the world, and it's obvious that you are in heaven.

*When living my free will....*

This means that because you are in heaven, you are finally free to make a choice. You recover your will, and the moment your will is free, you create a new agreement with life. You make the choice to live in communion with God because this is what is in your heart. It's not because your religion says you have to be with God. It's not because you are afraid. It's not the choice of the ego or the social image. It is *your* choice, your decision, because you *want* to do it.

When the real you makes a choice, you will not choose fear, envy, anger, drama, or anything that goes against yourself. Again, if you choose to live this way, it's not the real you who is making the choice. When you are living your free will, the only possible choice is God, is love, is happiness. Once you have the awareness of what you really are, your choice is to stay there, to be divine, to live in love the rest of your life.

*And with all the power of my spirit....*

This means that you support your decision with all the power of your will and your faith. This is the moment of your wedding with God, the moment of the fire initiation because your spirit is that fire; it is the divinity in you. First you recover your free will, which gives you enough power to make a choice, to make an agreement to live with God. Then you call upon all the power of your spirit to keep the agreement. Now you understand what you can do when you recover free will: You can handle intent with all the power of your spirit.

*I decide to live my life in free communion with God....*

This means you decide to live in love with God, with your divine self. This is your statement that you are crossing a line of no return, and making the commitment to God. Now you are in a committed relationship. All your faith is there; all your authority is there.

*With no expectations. . . .*

This means you surrender your attachment to the outcome because you don't know how anything will work out. You know that you are married to God; you know that you accept your own divinity. You detach from the outcome because the outcome is not important when you are committed to love. Living your life in free communion with God, you open your heart and love unconditionally. You love for no reason, with no expectations. Having no expectations, you give yourself, and you keep giving without expecting anything in return. Your love is unconditional because it is your pleasure to love.

*I will live my life with gratitude, love,*
*loyalty, and justice. . . .*

In this part of the agreement, you are telling your-self how you are going to write the story of your life. The decision is made, and now you express the form of your dream. This is how your life will look when you are expressing your creation, your art, to the rest of humanity. It is obvious how you will live your life, and you won't accept anything less than that because you are free, you are happy, you are love.

From now on, you will live your life with grati-tude, and it is easy to understand why. Gratitude is one of the most beautiful expressions of love. Just say-ing thank you will open all the doors to an abundance of life's blessings from all directions, but especially an abundance of love.

You will live your life with love, which means you

will love yourself unconditionally. You will accept yourself completely. You will respect and honor your physical body. No longer will you criticize or dislike what you are because you are God's creation. Your love is endless; the more you give your love, the more love you have to give. Love is your ticket to the kingdom of heaven, beginning with yourself, and continuing with your brothers and sisters.

You will live your life with loyalty. Loyalty to whom? To yourself, of course, which means that you will never do anything that goes against yourself; you will never betray yourself again. There is no place for self-abuse. You are loyal to yourself, and that makes you impeccable with your word.

You will live your life with justice, which means you are fair with yourself. If you make a mistake, you pay for that mistake, but only once, not every time you remember the mistake. To live your life with justice means you will no longer judge yourself, you will no longer live your life with guilt and shame. And when you live without judgment, guilt, and shame, there is no need to punish yourself.

*Beginning with myself. . . .*

This means that everything you have agreed to must begin with you. Living with gratitude, love, loyalty, and justice begins with you because you cannot give what you do not have. You can only give what you have. If you have love for yourself, then you can give love to others — in all of love's expressions. Living in free communion with God also begins by living in free communion with your divine self, as God's creation. The agreement always begins with yourself, and because this is what you are, this is what you share with others.

*And continuing with my brothers and sisters. . . .*

Now you start to spread the seeds of gratitude, love, loyalty, and justice to others. You live your life expressing love, and this is how you treat others everywhere you go. The love you have for yourself becomes the love you share with others. The seeds of love grow stronger, and they keep expanding until they become a beautiful relationship with your parents and children, your spouse and siblings — with everyone in your life. This statement gives you immunity to suffering because it ensures that every relationship is an act of love.

*I will respect all creation as the symbol of my love communion with the One who created me. . . .*

This means you will respect the forests, the oceans, the atmosphere, the animals — everything that God, your beloved, has created. You are expanding your love and respect to the entire world of creation as the symbol of your love and respect for the one who created you.

You make this agreement with God because now you recognize that everything in existence is God's creation. You respect God's will; you respect life as it is. You perceive God's creation, you respect creation, you participate in creation, and you surrender with total acceptance because you know that you cannot make it better. If you see a mountain, you do not say, "Oh, that mountain is in the wrong place, it shouldn't be there." No, the mountain is perfect the way it is, and you accept the perfection that exists within everything.

You don't need to change other people; you don't need to change any of God's creations. You simply enjoy the creation; you enjoy the beauty; you enjoy life. You are alive, and just to be alive gives you enjoyment. And what is the result of this?

*To the eternal happiness of humanity. . . .*

This means that all of humanity receives the benefit of your love communion with God. Since every human is part of one living being, the result of your happiness is the chance for all of humanity to live in happiness. You have decided to live your life in happiness, you are sharing your happiness with others, and the result is a wonderful gift to everyone around you. You are not responsible for the happiness of others; you are only responsible for your own. You are happy because you have a love communion with God. And if you can do it, everyone can do it, and the result of that union or reunion with God is the eternal happiness of humanity, which is another way to say "heaven on Earth."

The kingdom of heaven is your own mind, and for you, that kingdom is real, it is here, and you are part of that kingdom. You have a private kingdom of heaven in your mind, and by sharing it with your brothers and sisters, together you create the kingdom of heaven on Earth, to the eternal happiness of humanity.

***

Now you know the meaning of each phrase. But again, it's not enough to learn the words or to understand their meaning. It's about making this prayer your way of life. It's about the action. It's about practicing this prayer every day until you create heaven on Earth.

Many years ago, after finishing a cycle of teaching with my apprentices, we created the first Circle of Fire ceremony. The ceremony was for those who had recovered their will, their faith, and their love. All the people at the ceremony had experienced their divinity, but the challenge for them was to stay in heaven. They asked me, "Miguel, how can we stay there? Why do we have to come back?" My answer was, "You aren't staying in heaven because you still need to purify the mind. Your faith is powerful, but it is invested in what you believe you are, and most of what you believe about yourself is a lie. Take your faith out of the lies! Free your faith, and you will see how powerful you become."

If there is anything in your life that takes away your happiness, you have all the power you need to change it. You don't have to live with anger, or sadness, or jealousy. You don't have to judge yourself, make yourself guilty, and punish yourself.

Words and prayers are powerful agreements, and you need to see what kind you are using every day: "Oh Lord, I am guilty, I should be punished for my sins." What kind of prayer is that? If you believe you are guilty and deserve to be punished, you are asking for it!

Suffering and drama begin when you lie to yourself, even if you don't realize you are lying. You can recover the truth of what you really are. When you finally see yourself as you are, when you finally take responsibility for your creation, you will cleanse the lies from your own creation. You will free yourself from emotional drama by uncovering all the lies you believe in. It is a process of unlearning the lies. It is a period of cleansing, and it has nothing to do with the dream of society. How can we change the dream of society if we can't even cleanse the lies from our own dream?

"The Circle of Fire" prayer is enough for you to go to heaven and stay there. But first you need to take the agreement, live the agreement, and make it yours.

To say a prayer doesn't take more than a minute, but you need the discipline to do it. Say the prayer first thing in the morning when you open your eyes; then say it again before you go to sleep. Dream the prayer. Feel the prayer with your emotional body. Be the prayer; align your faith and intent with the prayer until your whole life is based on this prayer. If you betray yourself, then make a new agreement ... the day of the Lord ... and recover your free will.

Today is the most wonderful day of your life. This moment represents eternity. It is the moment when you return to love by deciding to live in communion with our Creator. Today is the day you agree to a new relationship, a matrimony with God. It is an eternal honeymoon, and that *is* heaven.

*❧*

## (Praying with a Group of People)
## THE CIRCLE OF FIRE

*[State today's date]*
*The day of the Lord*
*when the Divinity returns to us*
*when living our free will, and with all the power of our spirit*
*we decide to live our lives in free communion with God*
*with no expectations*

*We will live our lives with gratitude, love, loyalty, and justice*
*beginning with ourselves*
*and continuing with our brothers and sisters*

*We will respect all creation*
*as the symbol of our love communion with the one who created us*
*to the eternal happiness of humanity*

## (Praying in the Spanish Language)
## EL CÍRCULO DE FUEGO

*[Diga la fecha de hoy]*
*El día del Señor*
*cuando la Divinidad regresa a nosotros*
*viviendo con nuestra voluntad libre y con todo el poder del espíritu*
*decidimos vivir nuestras vidas en comunión libre con Dios*
*sin esperar nada en cambio*

*Viviremos nuestras vidas con gratitud, amor, lealtad, y justicia*
*empezando con nosotros mismos*
*y continuando con nuestros hermanos y hermanas*

*Respetaremos toda la creación*
*como símbolo de nuestra comunión de amor con el que nos creó*
*por la felicidad eterna de la humanidad*

Miguel Ruiz is the author of the international bestseller *The Four Agreements*, which has been translated into 27 languages. For more than a decade, he has worked with a small group of students and apprentices, guiding them toward their personal freedom. Today, he continues to offer his unique blend of ancient wisdom and modern-day awareness through lectures, workshops, and journeys to sacred sites around the world.

✥

For information on lectures and workshops
by Miguel Ruiz, please call
(800) 294-3203 or visit his web site:
www.miguelruiz.com

JANET MILLS IS THE EDITOR AND PUBLISHER OF AMBER-Allen Publishing. She is the author of *The Power of a Woman* and *Free of Dieting Forever,* and the editor of *The Seven Spiritual Laws of Success* by Deepak Chopra, an international bestseller with over two million copies in print. Her life mission is to inspire others to live the life of their dreams.

## THE CIRCLE OF FIRE IN A SONG

While this book was being prepared for publication, we discovered that a singer songwriter named Cari Cole had written music to "The Circle of Fire" prayer. Cari had been inspired to compose a series of songs after studying the teachings of don Miguel Ruiz and attending a power journey in Teotihuacan, Mexico.

Miguel has often said that the best way to master awareness and transformation is through repetition and practice, and we found that singing this beautiful prayer is a great way to make it a part of your life.

If you are interested in finding out more about Cari's music, please visit our web site or call us to inquire about purchasing a CD recording of her songs.

(800) 624-8855 · www.amberallen.com

### The Four Agreements

Based on ancient wisdom, The Four Agreements offer a powerful code of conduct that can rapidly transform our lives to a new experience of freedom, true happiness, and love. (Available in trade paperback, cloth gift edition, and Spanish language edition.)

### The Four Agreements Audio

In this unabridged reading of *The Four Agreements,* actor Peter Coyote gives powerful voice to the writings of Miguel Ruiz.

### The Four Agreements Cards

A beautifully illustrated, 4-inch square card deck containing 48 cards corresponding to each of The Four Agreements. A simple and powerful tool for transformation.

### The Four Agreements Companion Book

The *Companion Book* offers additional insights, practice ideas, a dialogue with don Miguel about applying The Four Agreements, and true stories from people who have transformed their lives.

### The Mastery of Love

Using insightful stories, Ruiz shows us how to heal our emotional wounds, recover the joy and freedom that are our birthright, and restore the spirit of play-fulness that is vital to loving relationships.

For a free catalog of Amber-Allen titles, call or write:

AMBER-ALLEN PUBLISHING

Post Office Box 6657

San Rafael, California 94903-0657

(800) 624-8855 · www.amberallen.com